Leadership

Expertise In Leadership Unleash Your Inner Leader: The
Definitive Resource For Becoming An Effective
Commander

*(How To Motivate Yourself To Perfection, Achieve Your
Goals, And Tap Into Your Inner Strength)*

Reinhold Kohler

TABLE OF CONTENT

Several Strange Associations Between Financial Success And Fitness

Only some haveOnly some have the physical attributes of a 6-foot 5-inch Olympic athlete. Still, we can compensate with our insights or sense of self, alternatively, somewhere along the usual dispute line, which might be more legend than fact.

Numerous studies suggest that taller men have a lower likelihood of being single or childless. This is likely due to the perception that taller men are more attractive to women and are, therefore, more likely to find love. As the famous saying goes, size counts when choosing a spouse. It's not that all successful men are naturally tall or attractive; in fact, many actors and inventors are relatively sharp or at least average in height.

1

Elaine Wong and colleagues at the University of Wisconsin studied pictures of fifty-five male leaders of large corporations and the profits for stakes. According to the study, businesses with heads that are wider than taller than their faces fare better financially. Leading executives from several well-known companies were present. Similarly, researchers at two premier research universities discovered that female CEOs of businesses were more attractive if there was less space vertically between their eyes and mouth than if it was more remarkable. These CEOs also had a higher chance of success.

Naturally, what relevance does this have to physical fitness? Are we suggesting that the only way to increase your income is through plastic surgery? Not at all, but your chances of succeeding in the business world are higher if you are physically fit. Numerous studies have demonstrated this, and although it is regrettable, it is something worth looking into and considering if you want to succeed in other areas of your life or at work. Let's examine some additional data and statistics regarding this correlation that are currently available.

Another significant study discovered that during brief encounters, people identify the identity traits of those who are physically attractive more accurately than others. The study revealed a positive inclination towards beautiful people. In the event that people perceive Jane as delightful, calm, and somewhat liberal, they will perceive her as more collected and liberal than she actually is. This is true even for those who exercise regularly, have a good build, and have control over other aspects of their lives like their weight. Experts argue that people are prompted to pay close attention to people who make them happy.

There are entire books written about the relationship between physical fitness and one's ability to advance in the business and financial fields. According to some researchers, it is a myth that engaging quality is subjective. They attempt to claim that magnificence is wholly arbitrary. Still, the majority of viewers view excellence in a comparable light. According to other researchers, less fit people are often disregarded, just like people who might be physically impaired or in need of learning support, and as a result, they are helpless against being separated. Thus, attractive people will have a better chance than less attractive people of finding employment and obtaining credit during a subsidence like the one we have been experiencing. This raises legal concerns because people who are less physically fit have a propensity to file lawsuits to recover lost wages. Naturally, this occurs frequently, and it's fascinating to observe the results; however, does the evidence support these conclusions, or are they just conjectured?

Successful people understand that there is a direct correlation between their personal and professional success and overall well-being. Consider a productive person you know for a moment. They work with a fitness coach, go to the gym on a regular basis, or get up a few minutes early to go for a brisk run. Successful people prefer to start their days full of energy and the happy hormones that come from exercise. Recent research has identified a direct relationship between achievement and well-being. Numerous studies published in recent years have specifically linked higher levels of wellness to improved ability to focus, increased trust, and improved ability to finish.

Additionally, a preeminent official investigation group examined over a thousand executives with annual incomes exceeding $100,000. When asked to describe their observations regarding weight and work, 75% of respondents stated that excellent physical health is essential for achieving professional success at the highest level. By contrast, only 17% of respondents thought that maintaining physical fitness was a worthy goal that came second to financial well-being. According to the CEO and organizer of that official hunt company, being physically well is a prerequisite for success in the workplace nowadays. Gone are the days when a little extra cushioning was a sign of growth and success. Almost 75% of executives who were given information regarding weight stated that being overweight is a natural barrier to their profession. Probably not, given our obsession with losing weight and the constant barrage of slender images that permeate popular culture. Instead, there is a robust correlation between increased well-being and increased productivity, as well as more incredible problem-solving skills, greater endurance, longevity, and energy, as well as decreased stress and weakness, all of which lead to better job performance.

It looks fantastic, but that's not all. Fit people tend to be more resilient to illness, which leads to improved eating habits and fewer missed workdays. Additionally, since competition is constantly growing across all industries, employers are now rewarding employees and managers who turn in more work and forget less. According to a study, after practicing, employees returned to work with greater self-acceptance and with a more remarkable ability to overlook their partners. The analysis happens to infer that "work execution was reliably higher, time administration abilities enhanced, as did mental sharpness." To experience these profits, all you have to do is put in roughly three or four half-hour to hour-long sessions per week. Consolidate quality preparation and cardiovascular activity alongside sound sustenance to rev up your mental sharpness, improve your gainfulness, lift your inclination, better oversee anxiety, and basically feel great. As your wellness level builds, your position on the stepping stool of achievement will as well.

other people's philosophies

People are what you work with. They share your nature and are just like you. They are individuals. They function in a given way and can be predictable. Their level of predictability is frequently directly related to how they view the world. A person's behavior is more predictable the more sensible they are. It's critical to identify this in other people.

The majority of people will attempt to impose their opinions on others. Realities can only be argued if that point of view is founded on correct assumptions. Regretfully, a lot of people in this circumstance could nevertheless attempt to make others do as they please. Interestingly, two significant worldviews that date back thousands of years and have influenced how we see the world today can be linked to their teachings.

ANTIQUE PHILOSOPHERS

Among the greatest thinkers in history are Aristotle and Plato. Plato was a teacher of Aristotle. While both individuals made many excellent remarks, we should concentrate on this one distinction.

Aristotle's teacher did not share his perception of reality. He thought that everything had a nature and could be known. His abbreviation for this was "A is A," which he named the Law of Identity.

In short, something is what it is. It is recognizable and has a specific nature. Thus far, we have discussed a reality-based approach. This is it.

Contrarily, Plato thought that the world and reality were but shadows. A cat was a reflection of the "form" from which all cats originate. We are unable to know what dimension this "form" resides in. Cats are merely various expressions of the "form" that is projected into the universe. He thought that the natural objects were located in a dimension separate from our own and that what we perceive is not accurate.

Recall that he lacked any concrete proof for this opinion. He was unable to produce any visible evidence or point to a "form." To explain what he felt needed an explanation, he put everything out of our reach and made it up.

The purpose of this is not to provide a philosophical history but rather to highlight these two radically divergent worldviews. One that is actual and another that is only a shadow alluding to an unknowable real world. Every day, we encounter these two points of view and their ramifications. This book does not aim to delve further into those schools of thought, but I recommend reading both giants if you are interested in learning more. This will do for us for the time being.

Is it possible to know and comprehend the universe? Or are they only shadows of reality, unreal? Your life and the way you live it are determined by the answers to these kinds of questions. You are not conscious of the manner in which these kinds of thoughts direct you. Getting them out in the open is a crucial first step. Try experimenting with it and consider the reasons behind your beliefs. Your surprise may be in the replies.

Capability 11: Perspective

Vision is ageless and embodies the overarching principles, convictions, and objectives of a group or leader. The strategies will adapt and vary throughout time, but the goal will never change. What counts most is the vision, which is the purpose.

It's simple to be sucked into the struggles of daily life. Remember the war. What is the team's vision? What is the objective? Complete the tasks pertaining to the final result. Consider whether this endeavor is advancing your goal. Refocus if not.

How strong is the vision?

A strong vision communicated by a capable leader is proof of conviction. It echoes through the strategies and shows the rest of the team that it believes in the image.

Those who share their convictions about the vision will be drawn to these influential leaders. The end product is a highly effective team committed to realizing the goal at all costs.

To be a good leader, you need to improve your communication abilities. You have to be able to articulate the vision clearly if you want to convey your conviction in it. Clearly and concisely stating the concept is the first step in effective communication. Make the idea something simple enough for anyone to comprehend.

Examine the following vision statements' effects:

Apple's goal is to create the world's most excellent personal computer.

Life is Good: The Contagious Power of Positivity.

Nordstrom: To provide the most engaging shopping environment for our patrons.

JetBlue: To uplift people everywhere, on land and in the air.

Together with a defined plan of action and direction, communication of the vision is essential. This is usually simple to accomplish when new team members join the mix. Bringing the present team members into the picture is a leadership opportunity.

How to help an existing team member succeed

To many of us, the word "change" is unsettling. It stands for ambiguity and uncertainty. Your approach to change has the power to decrease this dread. Transformation is associated with negativity; opportunity, on the other hand, is more positively interpreted. Change to the growth attitude of a leader.

Change—what is it? Evolutionary opportunities arise from change. Your team will grow more at ease with evolution as you do. When it comes to adapting to change, the team will look to you. The team is observing your reaction, including your nonverbal clues and vocal responses, just like in every other aspect.

It's crucial to remember that evolution is necessary for a business to thrive sustainably. Organizations that do not evolve will eventually fail to survive, maintain the status quo, and fail to introduce new items to the market. An excellent illustration of modern progression is AT&T.

Think about how ingrained this tiny piece of hardware is in your culture: the smartphone. When the Bell Telephone Company first started offering telephone services, switchboard operators manually connected consumers. The operator model eventually became unsustainable because of the number of clients. The dial phone in the home changed as the model became automated. The customer had the authority to get in touch with anyone directly, bypassing the intermediary.

The Bell Company changed with the times. AT&T acquired the Bell Company in 1983. This resulted in the development of cellular technology, enabling users to make phone calls while on the go. It isn't easy to fathom life without cell phones and applications in the modern world. Without AT&T, the cellular business would be very different today if the Bell Company had opposed the industry's progress.

There are several examples of executives leading a team through acquisitions, strategic initiatives, leadership changes, and even shifts in the company's mission throughout history.

It is your duty as a coach or leader to guide the group into new paths or evolution as a change agent. It would help if you influenced an organization in order to be a successful change agent, and this is accomplished through the multifaceted nature of trust.

So, how can one modify or grow a team?

Dale Carnegie created the most successful approach by imagining the future state and how you will guide your team to reach it.

My goal was to let everyone comprehend what it's like to lose, or almost lose, a life at our place of business. The audience members' facial expressions and the staff members' nonverbal body language made it very evident that they were giving the presentation their whole attention.

The second goal I discussed in my speech was to use this tragedy as a catalyst to alter our future work practices, priorities, and system of collective accountability for our safety as well as the safety of our coworkers. I gave a firm directive at the end of the meeting to pay special attention to and follow the established protocols in order to safeguard our company and ourselves.

"Everyone in this warehouse is special, unique, and essential to the success of our business," I said, reinforcing the idea. To be clear, though, I ask that you speak with your supervisor about resigning if you know of anyone in this warehouse who does not think they are affected by this message or who does not believe they can hold others and themselves accountable for their safety. Those who may step down won't be perceived as awful individuals; they're not a good fit for our company. Safety is important.

After calling the meeting to a close, I walked down from the platform to greet the staff. Many conversations were happening in groups that appeared to develop on their own. I received a lot of affirmation for the message I had sent while I mixed and listened. I was asked to join several group chats in order to inquire about the accident and John's condition. For a few weeks after the gathering, the most common response I received was genuine gratitude for the chance to gather everyone at once and hear a critical but forceful message.

More importantly, the steps that were taken following that discussion were evident from the marked increase in campus safety as well as the interpersonal relationships that I saw occurring there. We were safer and stronger because of the crisis.

An organization that operates as a collective living being occasionally has to disturb the status quo in order to establish focus and convey an obvious point. It's essential to use this approach sparingly to avoid it becoming the norm.

As a leader, you have to intentionally evaluate instances or circumstances as means of bringing about a necessary change and use them to advance the organization.

To unite an organization and concentrate on business objectives, executives might use a few key areas of concentration. Everyone should be able to comprehend and support a high emphasis on everyone's health, safety, and well-being.

Organizational leaders need to hone their feedback skills so they can provide employees with targeted advice.

The organization must hear the leader's heart, not simply their intellect.

It is a community that binds individuals together. A corporation needs a shared purpose, vision, goals, and strategic plan to have everyone pulling in the same direction.

Finally, there is Process. These are the specific guidelines, protocols, and standards that instruct individuals on how to behave and maintain order.

Recall that accomplishing consistent outcomes in accordance with a goal is the definition of control. A firm is an amalgam of different processes, each with plans that work together for the greater good.

After our talk this morning, David called to tell you about how a sales representative handled a large customer. Every problem needs to be viewed through the eyes of the three muscles. Is this sales representative working in the incorrect position? Or is he a decent man who needs to be made aware of National's goals, vision, and core principles? Is there a need for defined policies, procedures, or practices inside the firm that would consistently result in the desired behaviors?

Naturally, we need more data to evaluate this sales representative, but how much do you know about him?

Yes, I am familiar with him. He has been with us for a few years and is known for achieving his goals. He has worked in the veterinary pharmaceutical industry for more than ten years.

Why, in your opinion, did he take such a firm stance with a crucial client? Tom enquired.

The sales team has been under a lot of strain because our sales have yet to keep up with our expenses. We discovered that the way we paid commissions needed to be aligned. Less was being produced in commission for opening new accounts, and more was being paid for servicing current clients. This incentivized the sales representatives to prioritize their current clientele over acquiring new ones. We changed the sales compensation plan to address this and allow them to earn the same total revenue, but doing so required them to do more cold calls. Some representatives have suffered a decrease in pay as a result of their failure to rise. This rep would fit that description.

Tom reclined. That helps explain it, but it doesn't address the question of which muscle group is involved. Is this a flawed policy, a mismatch in values, or a weakness in character? Determining the issue becomes challenging when one needs to examine it through the lens of the three muscles. Community is the second muscle group, and since we can't psychoanalyze this bad rep this afternoon, let's talk about it.

The PVS, or Purpose, Values, and Strategy, comprise the community. I'm sorry to keep using so many acronyms. It's essential to keep them in mind. You will probably be discussing these topics. Therefore, you'll need to figure out how to explain the ideas clearly.

Counteraction To Self-Deprecating And Survival Lives Sincerity: A stool with three legs.

In reality, how can we be honest? I see three approaches to being truthful. God, other people, and oneself make up this triangle. It is necessary to cultivate and exhibit honesty in each of these three relationships. Being honest with God, ourselves, and others is an essential component of perfect honesty. It resembles a stool with three legs. What transpires in a three-legged chair when one leg breaks? The seat slips off.

Let's examine this using Psalms 26:1–8. It is acknowledged that David composed this while Saul and his troops were pursuing him specifically to defame him, portray him as a villain, and damage his reputation in Israel in order to prevent David from challenging King Saul's kingdom. How does David respond, then? What is his reaction to these unfounded allegations and the witch hunt? He starts by asking God to assist him in self-examination (v 1-3). After talking about other people and his company (verses 4-5), he ultimately acknowledges his relationship with God and the necessity of going to God's altar and sanctuary in order to find relief (verses 6–8).

Recall that being honest means not lying to oneself, others, or even to God. Deceit is the antithesis of honesty. To be righteous is to not lie to ourselves or other people.

It entails being truthful with oneself. Thinking more about who you actually are does not equate to being honest with yourself. It isn't arrogant and haughty. It is not to boast about one's abilities. It has nothing to do with overly confident self-perception, as corporate motivators would have us think. It is about accepting who we are and remaining modest. David acknowledges that he falls short of his God's expectations.

Because no one alive is righteous in Your eyes, do not judge Your servant (Ps. 143:2).

Being true to oneself means acknowledging one's weaknesses and getting support to overcome them. When we are sincere with ourselves, we recognize and respect who we are, as created by God. The other side is inhabited by those who live lives of self-abasement and survival. They enter a state of self-deprecation when they deny that God has given them any aptitude at all, rendering them useless in the eyes of God, other people, and themselves. They belittle their justifiable accomplishments. They reject the gifts that God has given them and refuse to use them. It's a mocking of modesty. I recommend this to them. They ought to attempt to state something like, "I can serve as a poor example; I'm not completely useless." God is asking us to be sincere with ourselves and to ask for His assistance when we are unable to understand who we are. David calls on God's grace rather than pleading with him to forget his shortcomings.

For Your righteousness' sake, O LORD, remember me not in my youth's sins or my transgressions, but in accordance with Your mercy (Ps. 25:7).

While we can't claim to be faultless or virtuous, we may be truthful and avoid being hypocrites. Let us beg God to search, judge, vindicate, and defend us, just as David did. Let us recall these passages, which contain David's supplication.

O LORD, declare me blameless because I have behaved honorably and have placed all of my trust in him. LORD, put me on trial and question me from both sides. Test my heart and my motivations. (Psalm 26:1-2, New Living Translation, NLT)

Being honest with other people is the second leg of the three-legged stool. This has two facets to it. Being open and truthful with people can be challenging. Every Sunday morning, I dread being asked the terrible question, "How do I look?" by my wife Leslie. The truth is that she looks excellent in everything and is always attractive. However, I'm still nervous about how I'm going to respond to her when she poses that query. She always says that I have no sense of style when I point out that anything needs to match or look better. That is true. She may claim that my compliments about her appearance are only intended to persuade her to get ready for church early. In this case, I am incorrect in any case. I am aware that their brides are asking one thing many newlywed guys fear, "Do I look fat?" If you are honest, you are doomed. I've heard that the appropriate response is to ask yourself, "Do I look stupid answering that question?" Jokes aside, it's not easy to be honest with people. Let's start by examining what being honest with others does not entail. It can occasionally be harmful to speak the truth about someone else. Sometimes, it can cause severe injury to others. Unrestrained candor can be detrimental. Telling the truth in love is mandated by the Bible.

The Diverse Categories Of Workers

The compulsive worker

He's always connected, constantly aware of what's going on, and always prepared to answer emails, even at odd hours of the night. He is exact and thorough— sometimes too much so—and can eventually become tiresome.

Please make an effort to assign him tasks that will keep him active all the time. Putting him out of work is the worst thing you can do with a resource like this.

2) The slobbering

Regardless of the choice you make, he consistently supports you. He extends his availability to you, frequently attempting to assist you personally. His sole objective is to leave a positive impression on you and every other employee in the organization; he is not in favor of teamwork.

Make it plain to him that having this mindset on your team will only get you somewhere by asking him to voice his thoughts frequently before listening to yours and adopting firm stances.

3) The labor activist

He is prepared to react with a citation from an article in the current collective agreement, regardless of the kind of work you assign him. For the sake of one more meal ticket, he would sell off his mother.

Avoid putting yourself in awkward situations and only write down orders or work instructions if you are positive there is no chance that they may be contested. Take caution to refrain from delegating to him projects that he has already completed or jobs that are above or below his level of expertise.

4) The astute

He has a remarkable capacity to highlight the little that he does, but he wants to do something other than work. 'Minimum effort, maximum outcome' is his philosophy. He is always the first in line when there are shortcuts available in any field.

If that attitude were to be rewarded, it might set a poor example for the rest of your staff. It's a nasty weed that must be pulled up before it gets bigger.

Try giving him more challenging assignments. Please verify that all pertinent information has been included in his work and that it has been completed to a high standard.

The impolite

Starting a conversation with a resource like this is challenging. She frequently veers toward becoming personal in her abuse or raising her voice in response to even the slightest sign of confrontation.

You won't succeed if you try to intervene by trying to modify his attitude or take control of the issue. You can't do much to combat ignorance, so there's no point in insisting and getting angry.

It would help if you strived to keep your cool and never come near him. Play it down now and then in an attempt to get a little confidence that will help you build a strong rapport and steer clear of awkward situations in front of others that can damage your authority.

Sixth, the yes man

Always consistent, with the ability to adopt one stance and then adopt the exact opposite stance five minutes later.

He is the worst employee you could have since he makes no effort to increase the productivity of the team.

When things go wrong, he will be the first to abandon you or flip on you; he will flatter you opportunistically and dishonestly.

Avoid them at all costs, and make it clear to them right immediately that you will never tolerate their attitude.

Instead of surrounding yourself with flatterers who merely want your praise, surround yourself with intelligent and driven individuals who will continually foster your growth.

Mirror the other person's conduct.

When talking with someone whom you wish to influence, employ the mirroring approach to be loved by the other person. To utilize this strategy, you first examine the minor mannerisms of the person you are talking to. Some people, for instance, like to cross their legs in a certain way. Others tend to touch their hair when they are worried.

You observe the tiny things that the individual whom you are talking to is doing. After a few minutes, try to mimic the gesture or mannerisms. Also, make sure that the other person is looking at you when you do it.

When you duplicate another person's gestures or actions, you are expressing that you have commonalities with that individual. The person you are talking to will think of you as relatable, and it enhances the possibility that they will follow what you are saying.

Influence individuals based on their need to believe

Humans are created with the impulse to believe. This is the reason why most people continue to follow religions even if there is no proof that supernatural creatures exist. People are mentally built to have a sense of belief in whatever they are passionate about.

One example of a need to believe is our urge to find a good leader to follow. Certain types of personalities prefer to follow rather than lead. If you only build an image of an ideal leader, you will be able to win over these personality types. This is the reason why giant corporations regularly change their CEO amid challenging economic periods. The new leadership fosters hope in the hearts of the workforce. The increased hope is more likely to motivate individuals to keep themselves motivated.

Your timing in accepting the leadership role is vital if you want to produce this type of effect among the people you lead. Steve Jobs, for example, returned to Apple while the Mac was struggling against rival PC brands. His reintroduction to the leadership role inspired hope among long-term Apple employees. This culture also offered them the chance to hire additional engineers for product development.

An excellent time to take a leadership role is when the present followers are discontented with the current leadership. If you enter the firm or the organization during this moment, even little victories will be perceived by your followers as big wins for the group. This will inspire them even more to achieve better.

You can sustain the faith of your followers with timely wins for the organization. After winning a few modest conflicts with your group, they will be confident enough to take on more demanding challenges.

He may also produce a leader out of an ordinary man and even be a great leader himself from being a common man previously. He merely needs to inform the individual with many more examples and other sorts of stuff that may inspire the man. He can urge the man to make a new start and motivate him to continue with his "never give up" mentality. He can not only become a man of tremendous leadership but also a man with a great vision, which he can combine into a man.

Good leaders can have a limitation of work, but a great leader does not have any limit. He can successfully produce a leader, which a competent leader cannot. He can also sense the potential in other men and may bring that potential out with his selfless approach. He can also guide the man out of the troubles he is facing, but a good leader can only do this for himself.

This explanation and examples clearly indicate that anyone who wants to be a leader needs first to sort out the attributes of a good leader and a great leader. That regular man who aspires to become a leader should also grasp that a good leader is the one who can 'keep' and a great leader is the one who can 'create.' For example:

Example C: There is a man who is the captain of a basketball team. His team is known for good performance, and he is the one who is a champion himself. He maintains the team's record by winning games with the support of other players supplied by the academy. There is another champion team whose captain is the man who believes in producing a new player to fulfill the need to sustain the team's record. He shows trust in the new players to become regular player for his team and inspire them to attain the success targeted for the team.

This example illustrates the story of two good players and two exceptional leaders who can 'keep' as well as 'create' in their respective domains. So, to become a leader, the new player would be eligible to perform, and as a new player, he would steadily gain experience and will have the power to compete even with his creator one day. He needs to follow the example of that great leader and become a player with the potential of a captain. This guy would undoubtedly give the credit for producing a good player out of him to the fantastic leadership quality of his captain, who exhibited incredible faith in him.

On the other side, a good leader can be a winner but cannot replace the absence of a great leader. He can be a man to lead from the front and perform many remarkable things by himself but not through the other man. For that reason, he is only a good leader and could be a better one. To become a great leader, he should have the capacity to 'make' another leader from a regular guy. If he could have done so, he would have also been described as a great leader, but regrettably, he is not the great leader here. He can only keep on with his current squad but not do anything essential to develop a man who can fill the legacy after his retirement. So, he is just an ordinary man here who has become a competent leader but not a great leader.

As a good leader, he can maintain his name in the golden words of the pages of history, but for the ones whom he has guided, he will be merely a good name worthy of remembering. On the other hand, a great leader does not need to be labeled by his name. He lies much above the idea of just being recognized as a name in history. He is more than a name; he is an icon and an inspiration. Even after his death, he remains a source of inspiration for many.

The harder-working and superior employee will eventually grow resentful and speak up.

Because we all have the mentality that no one enjoys a tattletale, the incompetent supervisor or the poor leader will then punish the employee for bringing up this other individual. Therefore, even though the issue did not originate between the two employees, we penalize the individual who exposed the other employee. The root of the problem was a poor leader who misattributed credit and needed to keep track of who was putting in extra effort and who wasn't.

It's interesting to see how a poor manager may incite hatred, force the better employee to go, and then be left with barely 10% of the workforce after making multiple such decisions. They are left with a team of workers whose combined efforts aren't worth the loss of one of their fired workers due to resentment. We want to keep an eye out for team chemistry early because of this.

There are a few easy steps you may take to make sure you are not one of these evil leaders. Start by outlining each person's function in detail, as well as the roles of each team and the organization. We've already talked about this by outlining expectations for employees, their duties, and the company's mission. Still, we also want them to understand how their roles relate to those of others.

Upon receiving their work description, a new hire may occasionally feel, "This is what I am supposed to be doing." However, one of your ten percenters, or longer-tenured staff members, will say, "Hey, I need you to work on this."

"It's not in my job description," the new hire will protest.

They will begin to transfer work to the new hire by saying, "Well, yeah, but this is what the last person who had your job did; this is your job."

You see it once the new employee completes the task and hands it to another employee, who then gives it to you. That is different from what you want to happen; instead, you want to keep an eye out for situations where workers take advantage of new hires or transfer their tasks to others. You must specify exactly who is responsible for each type of task.

It is tempting to assign one of your staff members more work. Sometimes, you want to give someone who excels in one area more responsibility in another, but doing so takes them outside of their area of competence. My transcriptionist is exceptionally talented; she can write well and quickly, and I could give her a lot of other jobs to work on, but she also does a fantastic job as a transcriptionist. She is as near to a perfect worker as I have ever encountered in the transcription department. She would, therefore, be operating at ten percent less than her typical efficiency if I brought her to work in editing, writing, or any other area where she is at ninety percent. The same is true when it comes to coming up with ideas for my social media person or collaborating with my assistant or head researcher. You may be rewarding good conduct when you assign them extra jobs that include interacting with other departments, but when you go beyond their scope of work, you run the risk of causing issues.

Eye Contact at the Appropriate Level

Making too much eye contact can make you appear uneasy and spooky. If you say too little, you come out as distant and unfriendly. Developing a precise quantity of eye contact is essential to increasing one's charisma. It's crucial to maintain appropriate eye contact with everyone you speak to in a social situation. Making eye contact demonstrates to the other person your importance and deserving of your time and consideration. Maintain eye contact, but avoid giving the impression that you're intimidating them by looking them down. Maintaining eye contact with someone is best done by keeping your attention on them for one second longer than usual. Similar to smiling, practice this in front of a mirror at home until you are satisfied with how you look.

Emotional Intelligence in the Workplace

Ever since Goleman's work brought emotional intelligence to the public's attention, there has existed a subset of the population that has become especially interested in the potential benefits of EQ. The corporate workplace, or the business world, is that section. Hiring managers and C-suite executives around the globe are eager to take advantage of emotional intelligence's advantages. Emotional intelligence in the workplace did not appeal to the baby boomer generation in general. All they did was work, pick up their compensation, and leave for home. The workplace of today is different. Younger workers want more from their jobs than just a paycheck.

The UK-based recruiting firm Robert Walters conducted a poll among millennials to learn more about different facets of their careers and jobs. The recruitment firm was able to infer from this poll that millennials are driven by entirely other factors than those that went previous generations. The millennial generation will not accept a job to have a job. Instead, people are looking for work that fulfills a greater purpose. They desire a sense of fulfillment and personal development. They want a sense of belonging to a larger community. The workforce of millennials also desires the liberty to arrange their work schedules without experiencing a sense of surveillance. They like the ability to interact socially with coworkers. They want work/life balance or a life away from the workplace. In addition, they want to be recognized, promoted, and paid more for the work they do.

Millennials have set a very high standard when compared to previous generations. Hiring managers are often plagued by insomnia as they attempt to ascertain which candidate is the most suitable for their organization. It should go without saying that IQ alone is no longer sufficient to influence employment decisions in light of this dynamic environment. Hiring managers are more influenced by emotional intelligence, even if they still prefer to employ intelligent applicants. Indeed, in a Harris Interact for Career Builder poll, 75% of hiring managers stated that they would like to work with someone who is emotionally intelligent rather than someone with a high IQ. This is not to say that hiring managers around the globe are all the same in their devaluation of book smarts. Instead, it demonstrates that businesses have finally realized that in order to thrive in today's workplace, knowledge of books alone is not enough.

Self-Restraint And Self-Management

The gist of this is actually relatively straightforward. You are continuously interpreting the situation, whether it is something that is happening in front of you or something that is coming from the past. You realize, as the reader, that you are far more in control than you think. You read with intent.

Meaning can indeed be subjective. Yes, I acknowledge that, but don't minimize the significance of emotional reading because circumstances might not be as dire as you recall. Things may not be as bad as you think they are right now.

Prevent the Loop of Negative Feedback.

Due to negative feedback loops, this becomes practically seductive, given our tendency to read the worst into our everyday behaviors. We find ourselves in a position where we wind up feeding back the worst interpretations of our simple stimulus. That need not be the case.

Positive feedback loops indeed exist. It is your choice to change the narrative. Alternatively, you may draw an upward spiral rather than a descending one. But it's a decision.

Regretfully, it takes work to exercise that option to know when and how to do it, and you have to see many failures until you get proficient at it. Nevertheless, you have to do it. In the alternative, a negative feedback loop results. This is the process by which shyness solidifies.

It grows bigger and stronger because you believe that reality has confirmed it. In fact, all you're doing is participating in a vicious cycle of feedback. You had an alternative to make. Things were possible to turn things around.

This is how it typically operates. You concentrate on how poorly you interpret the comments.

For instance, you might witness this beautiful person of the other sex acting in a way that seems to be intended for you. You provide it with the lowest possible negative reading. You take it to mean that everything about you as a person has been wholly disregarded, condemned, or rejected. You experience extreme unattractiveness, rejection, unloveability, etc.

You then experience shyness as a result of wanting to avoid social situations because you believe you will receive the same kind of response from them. As a result, you could do better. This could be simply leaving the social gathering, or it could be going there and sipping a beer while seeing everyone else enjoying themselves. On the other hand, you're merely dancing in circles by yourself or with your select group of pals if you're at a dance club or an outdoor celebration.

Unfortunately, this gets more nasty comments. At least you perceive them as unfavorable. People are going to sit up and take notice. After that, you read it in the worst possible light once more. This cycle of negative emotional interpretation keeps you going further and deeper into a hole.

In this situation, how do you think your shyness is handled? It continues to become stronger. In essence, what you're doing is telling yourself, again and over, that there is something wrong with you and that social situations are awful for you. It hurts you and makes you feel unloved and unwanted.

Here's some excellent news. You're not required to do it. You don't need to remain in that vicious cycle of feedback.

R: Give It a Justification

Give a justification for each task that is introduced, mainly if their enthusiasm has remained strong. What motivates us to do this? What does that mean, exactly? How does the family benefit from it? It is unreasonable to anticipate your child to engage in meaningless activities. They are not going to do anything "because I told you so," as they are extremely wise and educated sages. In the Bhagavad Gita, even Krishna attests to this: your highly evolved spiritual offspring will shun meaningless rituals.

Find out from them if their excitement has diminished. Do you need help finding this to be very annoying? Why are you not fond of it? You might discover that their fine motor skills need to be developed enough to know how to remove the toothpaste from the nearly empty tube or that the peppermint in their toothpaste is exceptionally awful. You may learn that they're not sure how to use hot water for dishwashing and that they prefer to use cold water. The to remove the trash may be hidden beneath numerous other boxes, and getting to them would require too much travel. Even though they might not even be aware of their hesitation, you can still resolve the issue and revitalize the Zen state connected to this service by working with them, traveling through the procedures with them, spending time in their company, and listening to their justifications.

V: Adjust the Task by Providing Options

Offering alternatives is a crucial strategy for getting your child involved in the tasks. Give your kids the freedom to decide what's best for the family, themselves, and you. Learn to recognize guided options like a pro.

Unfortunately, there are not many options available to youngsters in today's world. Children at school receive instructions on what to do and how to do it every thirty to forty-five minutes. All pupils, regardless of their interests or personalities, learn the same subjects and must pass standardized examinations to demonstrate their understanding, much like robots who only work at desks. Their desire for agency and free will is crushed by it.

Since not everyone can attend alternative, choice-based schools, let's make sure that we meet this vital need while we're with them. You'll provide them with a wide range of options. Have faith in your perceptive youngster to use reason and good judgment.

Certain parenting ideologies advocate for complete autonomy and minimal structure, while others advocate for strict rules and direction. A mix of all these ideologies is found in Bhakti, the traditional parenting philosophy that transcends the limitations of the most recent trends in child development. It requests that parents consider their child's individual needs as well as the expectations they have for them. Select options that satisfy both your and their demands. Additionally, please make sure the selections align with the leadership traits you envisioned in Level 1 and that they are acceptable to you. (For instance, if you want them to learn selflessness, don't give them a selfish option.)

Their choices will reveal the kinds of activities they enjoy. You'll be able to expand on those choices and start helping them find their calling. You can start with this list.

An Eager Heart Looks For Chances Everywhere.

There Might Only Be One Position Available, Depending On The Demands And Size Of A Fire Station. However, Two Realities Always Remain The Same: There Will Always Be More Applicants Than Open Positions, And There Will Always Be More Unhappy People Than Satisfied Ones. A Large Number Of People Whose Names Were Not Selected For Employment Will Be Listed As Eligible. But, During The List's Average Six- Or One-Year-Long Duration, There Is No Assurance That Anyone Will Be Hired. This Implies That The Applicant Has To Begin The Application Process Anew Whenever The Eligibility List Expires. Ask Any Fireman About Their Hiring Process, And You'll Find That A Large Number Of Them Went Through The Procedure More Than Once Before Landing A Job. These Are The

Firefighters Who Never Gave Up Despite Constant Setbacks.

However, Joe Schmuckatelli's Work Continues Even After He Receives The "Congratulations! We're Giving You A Job Offer Because You Made It. That Job Offer Is Conditional And Dependent On Joe Passing A Background Investigation And Medical Screening. When Doctor Death Concludes That Joe Is Well And Does Not Have A Persistent Toenail Fungus, Everyone Waits To Hear The Results Of The Background Check. At Last, Joe Finds Out That Everything Is Fine And His Record Is Spotless. He Is Content And Moves On. Occasionally, Though, The Physician May Discover A Severe Medical Issue That Disqualifies A Candidate, In Which Case They Are Not Considered Any Further. The Ugly Head Of Disappointment Rears Up Once More.

In This Case, Joe Passes With Flying Colors And Enrolls In The Fire School, Which He Attends For At Least Three Months. A Recruit May Be Expelled From The Academy On Occasion For

Behavioral Issues, Physical Or Academic Failure, Or Other Causes. I'm Disappointed. While Some Will Move On To Another Field Of Work, Others Will Begin The Application Process Anew.

Buyer Caution! The Former Firefighter Who Had Their Ambitions Crushed On The Rocks And Failed The Academy Might Be Your Next Hire At Electrifying Energy. You Might Be The One Who Makes A Big Difference In The Person's Ability To Move Past Their Negative Experience As The Leader.

At Last, The Day Of The Fire Academy's Graduation Approaches. Joe Stands In Front Of His Peers, Family, And Other Firefighters. As The Fire Chief Pins Their Well-Earned Medals On Their Chests, They All Beam With Pride. In A Few Days, Each Of Them Reports To The Fire Station They Have Been Assigned To, Where They Will Begin A One-Year Probationary Term That Will Involve Additional Training And Study.

At Some Point, FirefighterSchmuckatelli Wants To Advance Through The Ranks

And Turns His Attention To The Future. Perhaps Unexpectedly, The Fire Chief Doesn't Just Stroll Into A Station, Point At Joe, And Declare, "You're Now A Lieutenant!" In Public Safety Agencies, Promotions Are Typically Obtained Via A Demanding And Taxing Testing Procedure. For A Restricted Number Of Roles, This Means Further Research, Testing, Preparation, And Interviews. Those Who Are Promoted Feel Relieved That The System Is Over And Are Happy, Joyful, And Satisfied. Those Who Were Not Promoted Are Disappointed At Having Been Overlooked. Before Getting Promoted, A Lot Of Them Will Attempt Twice, Three Times, Or More. Some Give Up On The Chase Altogether. Some People In The Latter Group Might Grow Resentful.

I've Seen All Sides Of The Issue. I Was Thrilled And Ecstatic To Hear From The Fire Chief When I Got The Job, And I Felt The Same Way When I Got Promoted Later In My Career. Additionally, I Was Disheartened And Upset Following A

Promotion Rejection. It's A Tale Reminiscent Of The World Series Previously Told. The Houston Astros Were Bouncing Up And Down And Piled On Top Of Each Other On One Side Of The Field. They Were Overflowing With Gladness And Joy.

Conversely, The Los Angeles Dodgers Were Defeated And Heartbroken. A Fantastic Range Of Feelings From Happiness To Sadness. Our Level Of Expectation And Level Of Preparation Directly Affects How Hard We Land.

As A Recruiter, You Will Probably Run Against Other Derailers, Mainly If You Act As An Internal Consultant. One Of These Is Low Customer Motivation, Which Is Typically Observed In Circumstances Where The Client Isn't Voluntarily Initiating The Contact. The Most Frequent Situation Involves A Client Being Under Pressure To Proceed With The Search Even Though They Disagree With The Way Their Supervisor Started The Recruitment Process. Recruiters Serving As Internal

Consultants May Get Around This Obstacle By Segmenting The Engagement Into Manageable Chunks. A Customer May Gain Momentum And Tiny Victories By Quickly Completing A Number Of Modest Tasks, Which Will Increase Their Motivation To Work On The Project. Creating A Helpful Feedback Mechanism That The Client Can Use To Provide Their Boss With Feedback Would Be Another Strategy You Could Use To Assist The Client In Appearing Good To Their Boss.

Consistently Providing The Client With Progress Updates And Maintaining Positive Communication Can Both Be Beneficial. Giving Your Customers Some "Skin In The Game"—That Is, A Certain Amount Of Ownership Over The Engagement Implementation Process— Is A Part Of Your Job As A Consultant. Low Client Motivation Frequently Arises From The Client Believing They Have Little Influence Over The Situation Or How It Will Be Resolved. Keeping The Client Moving Is A Common Strategy

Used By Recruiters To Get Beyond This Obstacle. Instead Of Trying To Evade Or Even Slow Down The Process, The Client May Realize That Momentum Is A Strong Force That Keeps Them Going.

Resistance Is Another Derailer That Recruiters May Encounter At Any Point In The Interaction. Resistance Occurs When A Project's Forward Momentum Wanes. It Can Manifest As The Client's Inability To Make Harsh Or Unpleasant Decisions, Their Increased Questioning, Or Their Persistent Need For Minute Details. Although Some Resistance Is Average, You Can Get Past It By Comprehending Its Underlying Causes More Clearly Since Emotion Is Frequently The Driving Force Behind Resistance; Likely, The Client Has Yet To Tell You About A Topic That Is More Important To Them And Is The Source Of Their Resistance. When Dealing With Resistance In Consulting Engagements, Please Make An Effort To Recognize The Different Kinds Of Resistance Occurring And Have A Neutral Conversation About

It With The Client. In This Approach, You May Set The Stage For A Fruitful Discussion With The Client.

• • •

While We've Discussed A Few Techniques, Abilities, And Characteristics, Issue-Solving Is A Dynamic Process That May Call For Minor Alterations As You Go. A Reasonable Conclusion Can Be Significantly Influenced By Your Willingness To Make Little Adjustments To Your Plan Of Action When Fresh Information Becomes Available. Leadership And Decisiveness Are Two Different Things. As A Change Leader, You Must Assist The Client In Making Decisions. Furthermore, You Must Help Them In Modeling This Shift In Their Leadership Position. Creating A Vision That Matters And Involving All Stakeholders Jointly Is More Critical Than Advocating And Uniting Around Ideas And Change Processes.

Having People Follow A Checklist Won't Increase Accountability; Instead, Concentrate On Fostering Responsibility And A Sense Of Connection To The Plan. Each Person Brings Unique Competencies To The Table; Your Job Is To Identify These And Use Them To Support Change Rather Than Attempt To Repair Things The Way You See Them. The Majority Of Factors That Matter In Bringing About Change Are Immeasurable, So Your Internal Client Strategy Must Take That Into Account. Change May Not Always Be Visible To You, So Be Careful To Look Closely For It And To Acknowledge Both Tiny And Large Victories. Recall That, As The Actual Gatekeepers Of The Organization's Future Leadership, Recruiters Play A Critical Role In Supporting Change Within Organizations. They Do, Nevertheless, Also Tread Carefully When Interacting With The Client, The Organization, And The Candidate. Even Though These Three Crucial Organizations Could Each Have A Distinct Focus And Set Separate

Goals, It Is Your Responsibility To Align Them All. The "Recruiter's Bizarre Life Triangle" Is What We Refer To It As.

"What's The Purpose Of This?"

As Ceo, President, Board Member, Or Facilitator, I Led Or Participated In Numerous Business Planning Sessions. Often, I Would Inquire, "Remind Me Again, Why Are We Doing This?" Regarding A Decision That Had Already Been Made. "I Thought We Already Made This Decision Weeks Ago," Would Be The Typical Reply. "We Did," I Replied, But Could You Maybe Repeat The Explanation? Using The Information At Hand, We Made Our Decision. Given What We Have Discovered Since Then, Let's Confirm That The Original Decision's Justifications Still Hold.

You Can Confirm The Arguments In Favor Of The Decision If It Is Still Sound. This Question Will Start The Necessary Dialogue If The Decision Has To Be Adjusted.

Nothing Is Unquestionably More Pointless Than Performing Quite Well, Which Ought To Be Avoided.

Peter Drucker (P.

The Sooner You Realize That Something That Was Previously Significant Is No Longer Relevant Or Requires Reconsideration, The Sooner You May Change It Or Give It Up.

Asking Yourself, "Why Are We Doing This?" And The Questions That Follow Help A Company Make Wise Decisions And Promote The Mental Health Of People Who Are Spending Time On Activities That Are No Longer Relevant. Furthermore, Posing This Query Will Foster A Culture That Embraces Deviations From The Norm.

This Is My Straightforward Motto For The Procedure:

Assemble Data. Assess. Choose.

Assemble Data. Assess. Adjust As Necessary.

Assemble Data. Assess. Adjust As Necessary.

Repeat Without Stopping.

Take Ownership Of It. Call It By A Name. Ask Your Group To Edit It So That It Can Be Used In Your Company. Mark Choices That Stand To Gain From This Process Of Continual Improvement And Schedule Frequent Follow-Ups.

When You Make A Prompt Adjustment Or Modification, You Will Have Reprocessed The Initial Decision. No Matter How Wise A Decision Seems At The Moment, It Can Constantly Be Improved.

This Strategy Allows For The Use Of Fresh Information From All Sources, Including The Decision's Current Outcomes. Rapid Adaptation In Dynamic Situations Is Supported By This Process.3. Additionally, It Makes Room For More Improvisation Because You Will Be More Adept At Responding When Dynamics Change The More You

Comprehend And Practice Them. Similar To Jazz.

The Organization Will Probably Surpass Others In The Long Run If The Adaptive Decision Improves The Outcome By Five Percent Or Even One Percent. An Even Stronger Scenario Would Be If The Initial Choice Were Entirely Supported By Evidence, Demonstrating The Leadership And Team's Ability To Make And Carry Out Decisions. Sixteen.

1. Learning The Art Of Business Improvisation: Https://Sloanreview.Mit.Edu/Article/ Learning The Art Of Business Improvisation: Https://Sloanreview.Mit.Edu/Article You Can Get A Printout At Http://Mitsmr.Com/1spz5dj.

3. I Initially Became Aware Of This Idea When I Studied The Observe-Orient-Decide-Act (Ooda Loop) Cycle. Colonel John Boyd Of The United States Air Force Is Credited As The Military Strategist

Behind It. Boyd Used The Idea To Describe Air Combat Activities, Sometimes Known As Aerial "Dogfights." In Similar Circumstances, Failing To Adjust In Light Of Fresh Knowledge Quickly Could Prove Fatal.

Main Conclusions:

We Went Over The Three Key Factors To Take Into Account When Deciding What To Learn In This Section. These Are The Following:

Degree Of Curiosity

Practicality And Promptness

Here Is A Synopsis:

1. Interest Level

The Selection Of Learning Material Should Be Engaging For You, Which Means Considering The Following Factors:

Enthusiasm. Learning About Topics You Are Interested In Is Preferable. If Not,

You'll Have To Rely Solely On Your Strong Will And Unwavering Self-Control. The Benefits Should Be Enormous To Make That Expertise Worthwhile If Your Interest Level Is Modest.

Fervor. Finding Your Greatest Passion Grants You Boundless Energy, Unmatched Perseverance, An Endless Sense Of Wonder, And A Great Deal Of Patience. When At All Feasible, Acquire Abilities That Genuinely Fascinate You.

Sensation. Avoid Concentrating On Making "Rational" Decisions When Learning. Instead, Make An Effort To Decide On Things That Inspire And Speak To You. As Humans, We Frequently Act On Our Emotions Rather Than Reason When Making Decisions.

2. Utilities

Learning Must Be Actually Beneficial, Which Means Taking Into Account The Following Factors:

The Degree Of Unity With Your Goal. Getting The Abilities You Need To Bridge

The Gap Between Where You Are And Where You Want To Be Is A Significant Part Of Learning. It Will Be Simpler To Determine The Abilities You Need To Acquire In Order To Realize Your Vision If It Is More Apparent.

Benefits. Every Action You Take Has A Cost Associated With It. A Skill Has To Be Very Beneficial In Order To Be Considered Valuable. It Needs To Support You In Achieving Your Life And Career Objectives.

Range Of Ability Or Expertise. Your Learning Must Have An Effect. That Is, It Needs To Provide You With The Momentum, Confidence, And Many More Options That You Need.

3. Promptness

The Current Context Of What You Choose To Learn Should Be Highly Relevant, Which Means Taking Into Consideration The Following Points:

What's On Your Plate Already? You Can Only Absorb So Much Information At

Once. Think About If You Can Add One More Talent At This Time.

Both Time And Energy Are At Hand. There's Only So Much Time And Energy You Have. Assess The Time And Energy You Have To Dedicate To Learning A New Skill.

Applicability Of The Ability To You At This Time. Make Sure The Skill Is Applicable To You Right Now Because Most Of The Stuff We Learn Needs To Be Remembered. Consider Learning It Later If You Can't Utilize It Right Away Or If It's Not A Top Priority.

Which Should Come First: The Egg Or The Chicken?

Was the actual necessity for the mouse, rather than the mousetrap, the cause for concern? Given that he knew where the mousetrap was, he may have avoided it recently. The most significant danger to him was that the snake might eat him. There may have been other snakes present as well. He should have made protecting himself from the snakes his top priority.

 To a certain extent, the damaged rancher did not really need to buy the mousetrap. His primary priority should have been to increase his source of income. A REAL-LIFE STORY:

Great pioneers understand what they need. If you look around, chances are good you'll see that everyone is busy. Perhaps you are too preoccupied. The question is, what are you caught up with doing? Are you preoccupied with carrying out your obligations or preoccupied with finishing tasks that you shouldn't have started in the first place?

Later on, there will be more significant activity in our world. We will have "less time" even with the introduction of the newest cutting-edge technology, which is meant to boost our productivity. There will never be "more time" for us. No matter what we want to do, we will only have 24 hours a day.

It is crucial to decide what you should be working on first as a result.

THE "EGG OR CHICKEN" METAPHOR

People frequently question, "Which came first, the chicken or the egg?" Our chicken and egg exercise allegory for prioritization deals with the tasks we choose to complete first. When it comes to concentrating on your workouts, ask yourself, "Which should come first—the chicken or the egg?" Another way to think about Chicken and Egg is differently. Chickens could represent the actions that give you gains in the near term. The egg can stand for fundamental tasks that set you up for future success. We must occasionally make difficult decisions, and since we only have 24 hours a day, we must make difficult decisions every day.

Arnold Bennett writes, "Which of us isn't saying to himself for his entire life: 'I will adjust that when I have somewhat more time'?" in his book How to Live on 24 Hours per Day. There will never be any more time for us. There is, and we always have, and we have had continuously.

This is the issue. That book was written more than a century ago. As a matter of fact, we are out of time and never will be again.

Arrange the day. Remember to set aside meaningful time to complete essential tasks. A top executive once informed me of a large international company that she would always make notes about her plans for the next day, including what she anticipated to accomplish and when. "Things don't go 100% according to my arrangements, but the daily organizing process makes me distinctly mindful of my needs," she added. I made more significant progress. I keep moving forward and don't turn around to see how nicely I set up the previous day.

Wait to start doing it as soon as you get up every day. Remember to inspect your arrangement and plan your day. In any other case, you might need more time to accomplish what matters to you.

The desire to do the right thing first is closely related to prioritization. In the unlikely event that you lack a concentration tendency, you can end up doing something that you shouldn't have done in the first place.

As you will see in the upcoming sections, more than setting priorities on its own is required. Still, setting priorities helps you stay aware of the limited amount of time you have available and keeps essential tasks at the top of your list.

For advice on organizing and setting priorities, see the Mousetrap Resource Center.

The 'monkey Story' And The Takeaway Management Lesson

Let's remember a well-known tale from our youth. A monarch once owned a monkey as a pet. The monarch had forgotten the monkey's fundamental characteristics and instincts, which must have been clear to him but that he ignored, and had instead constructed the preconceived notion that the monkey was smart enough to get him to serve as his bodyguard. It once happened that in the summer, the monkey was fanning the sleeping king. As the monarch slept, the monkey focused on tending to his needs according to its instincts and characteristics. It suddenly became aware that a fly was perched above the king's nose. After numerous attempts, the monkey made a valiant effort to remove the fly from the king's nose, but to no avail. Frustrated, the monkey snatched the king's sword and killed the fly by smashing it against the king's nose, allowing the king to resume his undisturbed slumber. It was a fly! There was a king! The king killed the monkey because he had a vague idea of its characteristics.

From a psychological angle, Genetic coding, or inheritance derived from parents, and subconscious mind training from life events and education are the two primary sources of personality traits. The characteristics are evident in both personal and professional spheres. Workers in all types of organizations will adhere to the same physiological and psychological guidelines. As a person matures on the initial architecture of their brain (from birth), the neurological components of their brain are rewired. Business organizations and corporations should avoid making snap decisions when forming teams and departments because these actions have an impact on how well the teams work together.

The entire goal of business growth would be undermined if corporate management did not consider this psychological idea while making decisions. If not, unpleasant, stunted executions may be avoided cleverly.

Corporate lesson: If the incorrect team is assembled—one that lacks the necessary skills and has just rudimentary knowledge and experience—project goals will never be achieved. Selecting a team is essential and ought to be done proactively.

A carefully thought-out plan is put into action because the hiring process is vital to the corporate or company organization. Typically, there is a one- to two-year gap between recruitment and joining. Following this time, students officially begin working as "trainees" in their respective organizations. Next, training is provided for the "trainee" (new hire) with consideration to the potential future contributions the trainee may make to the business community. If the students do not comply as anticipated, there is a loss in finishing the recruitment process. Some students have been seen to quit during the training session or a short length of service, and some have yet to join (as they sporadically seek other alternatives). That is a significant loss for the concerned company since the new hire's real contribution begins after receiving thorough training during that time. The protective measure Once the recruiting has been verified, the students who are still in their last year of education should be called to the company during institute/university holidays to receive supervised training. In this manner, only genuine students—those who genuinely want to join and are unlikely to leave the company in the near future—would come and participate in the growth of the corporation, which would also feature their development, saving the company from having to pay additional training costs after the employee joins the corporate. In this manner, we are able to provide competent, qualified experts to new hires while removing the "academic-organizational" integration gap!

From a psychological angle: Human psychology states that people consider possibilities constantly in order to choose the best one; however, this part of psychology has a drawback when it comes to organizational stability: people have a propensity to betray others when considering other options. To avoid any loss to the corporation, however, we should conduct psychoanalysis on any new hires (through the recruitment process) who appear to be a likely fit before adding them to the corporation in the near future. This psychoanalysis should be based on the corporate concept, organization behavior sustenance, and professional aptitude.

Business lesson: Test new hires before assuming they have the professional aptitude to contribute to the company. This is a screening principle that should be used for new hires. Only after a thorough examination can a new hire be qualified to join the business family.

Leading a Discussion

Human beings, whatever different we like to think we are, are similar in nearly every way. Once we recognize this, we may begin to take note of the essential qualities and ideals that drive us all. We may significantly increase our control over a situation and make our interactions stand out from the crowd by appealing to these fundamentals.

Asking questions is one of the best methods to guide discussions and relationships. Well-timed questions exhibit attention, knowledge, and intellect while simultaneously developing rapport and leading the encounter toward your intended conclusion. Making someone feel important is a fantastic spot to start your conversation and an excellent method to break the ice; begin by thanking your audience for their time, coupled with good eye contact and a genuine smile.

Using open-ended questions to lead a discussion takes practice; here's a few examples to get you started:

What is important to you outside of work?

How did you accomplish all that you have?

How could I gain your level of experience?

How did you feel about what happened?

What do you remember about the event?

What do you do to stay motivated?

Looking back, how would you have done things differently?

What are your recommendations for possible improvements?

How could the group become more effective?

Most open inquiries begin with words like what, who, where, and how and require more than a yes or no answer. These questions are designed to get people talking, and when people are talking……we are listening, learning, and obtaining a deeper level of understanding. Try to avoid should and would lines of questioning as these questions often require yes or no replies.

If you're the one being questioned, take your time and stop before you answer. Consider not answering the question if it will serve you better not to. Your delay will allow you time to write an adequately edited answer or to design a clever dodge. Instead of answering the question that you were asked, answer the question that you wanted to be asked. This strategy works remarkably effectively and exhibits strength of character.

Conflict

There are a lot of individuals living in this world, all living very varied lives with differing beliefs and interests. Throughout our lifetimes, we each construct our internal maps and tactics to help us survive and thrive in our tiny part of the earth. No two experiences are identical; this causes each of us to develop unique techniques for dealing with the environment, resulting in multiple solutions for each problem. When a team is faced with a decision, members may come into disagreement throughout the action to pursue, even when they have the same aim. Many strategies will work well and complement one another, but others may not.

How do we settle conflicts yet successfully attain our goals?

There are three common ways in which people usually deal with disagreement. Flight, fight, or give up are our obvious options, each having their intrinsic winning or losing results.

Flight

By avoiding conflict, we lose, and the situation may fester; no guarantee avoiding a conflict would address the issue. We may assign problematic decisions to other people, and they may produce a win for our team, but as individuals, we will need to gain both knowledge and experience.

Fight

Choosing to fight telegraphs one purpose: a desire to win openly. For us to win, another must lose. We must be triumphant. But even with our victory secured, is there a better way?

Give up

Giving up ensures one thing: we get nothing, and we lose.

Compromise

A compromise is often assumed to be the 'all-around' best option, but in reality, all sides must lose a little in order for the center to be realized.

A True Consensus

When we reject the typical win-lose concept, additional options begin to reveal themselves. Working in collaboration, numerous sides can generate new ideas superior to a compromise.

Don't be afraid to face issues directly, even if they raise unpleasant feelings within the group. It is always best to air and address any difficulties. Problems left unsolved decay over time, and when they finally come to the forefront, they will be far more challenging to deal with.

Classifying Mistakes

Mistakes happen in different shapes and sizes; we must classify them in order to keep everything in perspective and to learn everything we can from them. Generally speaking, individuals behave with good intentions, and mistakes are never personal. The three areas that are the source of most errors are a lack of competence, a lack of an exemplary method, or a lack of knowledge. With these three examples as the fundamental causes of errors, if a mistake is made, it can usually fit into one of the following three categories:

Mind slip: When the correct process is followed, but one aspect of the process needs to be included, accurate, or adequately completed.

General human error: When the customary method is not correctly followed.

Genuine mistake: When no process or the improper process is attempted.

Resolution

What needs to change from here? Is it a procedure, training, or an environmental issue?

What was the intention behind the mistake?

What have we learned via this experience, and how has it strengthened our understanding?

Implementing Change

Define the reasons for and the values crucial to the change and list them in order of significance; this will offer you further insights into the finer elements of both the required adjustments and the best techniques for implementing and sustaining them.

How will you identify that the change has been successfully implemented?

You must write out your strategy for change, as well as the minor goals or signal posts that will allow you to assess your success.

When establishing your strategy, pay close attention to any potential risks and make preparations for several conceivable scenarios, each ensuring your victory.

Request support from those around you. To fully implement a change, everyone must be in accord. Work on being able to communicate the reasons for and the advantages of the difference within 3 minutes. Your summary should be persuasive enough to motivate your team and cement your coalition for change.

Are You Awarented Of The Goals Of Your Talents And Gifts?

God has endowed every one of us with special skills, aptitudes, and capabilities. The issue is, how can we use them effectively? Understanding your comparative advantage and developing your vision is essential to using your gifts and talents for God's purposes. However, it also entails understanding the "how" and "why" of using these gifts from God in our daily lives.

Unfortunately, the post-modern notion that each person should select their own set of life principles that work for them—do what seems best to you—has led to a growing number of people taking a relativistic approach to living. The idea that "I can do whatever I need to in order to get what I want" is propagated by today's popular culture, which holds that "the ends justify the means." Indeed, this is not a novel idea. The statement "everyone did what was right in his own eyes" appears at the end of the book of Judges (Judg. 17:6). As Christians, we have to reject this fallacious approach and accept the biblical teaching that sets forth guidelines for all we do. (Matt. 5:17–18, Rom. 7:12, Ps. 119:96, Ps. 19:7). Jesus provided a summary of moral principles in Matthew 22:36–40.

In his letters, the apostle Paul clarifies that legalism originates not from deeds but from motivations. Legalism arises whenever we attempt to impose our own or others' ethical standards on someone by following the letter of the law. The idea of virtue in the Bible comes from God's nature. Christians have Christ as their role model for virtue, and the Holy Spirit is the source of virtue in the believer. As God writes his laws on our hearts through the Holy Spirit, virtue develops in the framework of the spiritual life (2 Cor. 3:3, Heb. 8:10). As a result, we cease abiding by the law in an effort to establish our righteousness. Because we love the one who has made us righteous, we start to obey. Realizing that our gifts and talents must be used within the framework of a moral and virtuous life is the first step towards employing them appropriately. However, we are not obligated to live moral lives in order to look down on others or to satisfy God with our righteousness.

Section Three

BROKENESS AND THE LEADER

A glass drops to the ground and shatters into a million pieces. It instantly loses all value and gets thrown away. In the real world, the value of a broken item drops right away.

But the reverse is true in our spiritual existence. We are more valuable to the kingdom the more broken we are. Compared to unbroken leaders, broken leaders do significantly better.

What does brokenness really mean? It is a complete submission to Jesus Christ's lordship, recognizing His authority as ultimate. It entails letting go of my egotistical need always to get my way and accepting that Christ's way is the best. Actually, what I am calling brokenness is called death in the Bible. Nevertheless, I have chosen the phrase brokenness because no one wants to read a chapter called "The Leader and Death." Luke uses the following language to describe Jesus' teaching on brokenness:

Then he addressed everyone, saying, "If anyone wishes to follow me, he must daily deny himself, take up his cross, and follow me." Because whoever sacrifices their life for me will save it, but whoever seeks to preserve their life will lose it. Even if a guy were to acquire everything in the world, would he still lose or forfeit himself? When the Son of Man returns in his glory, together with the glory of the Father and the holy angels, whoever is ashamed of me and what I have said will have the Son of Man ashamed of him. (Luke 9:23-26)

The Anticipation Of Fragility

Jesus discusses a level of Christian experience in this text that only some of His disciples stop to think about. He talks about living a life in complete submission to His lordship, sacrificing your entire life, and giving up everything you hold most dear.

Because of how radical His teaching is, we frequently write it off as a message intended solely for a small portion of His followers. However, Jesus wants us to understand His message. He addressed "them all" and said "whoever" and "anyone who would come after me." He is aiming His criticism at all of His disciples, not just a chosen few. He is addressing everyone who wants to be a follower of His. Every disciple is expected to go through this brokenness experience with Him. Jesus was aware that people would not embrace this teaching. After telling His disciples to "deny yourself and lose your life," He did not anticipate (or get) a resounding "amen." However, He did not back down from outlining His expectations in detail. You are engaging in cheesy discipleship if you disobey Christ's command in this text.

When you hear Jesus tell you to "go into all the world and preach the gospel," you obviously feel less frightened than when you accept his invitation to be broken, to die to yourself, and to give up your life. Your body resists giving up at all costs. Nevertheless, Christ's expectation endures. Will you agree to His terms or not?

The Brokenness Experience

Let's examine Jesus' teachings in more detail. What does He mean when He talks of death and brokenness? In what ways will you apply this to your own life?

Brokenness calls for demise.

Jesus starts by teaching us that death is the only option for those who are broken. "Take up your cross," he commands. The cross has yet to be well known in today's culture. The only instances of crosses that we come across are as religious symbols in images or as necklace jewelry.

However, the disciples were fully aware of his meaning. They were aware that there was only one purpose for the cross: DEATH. Although there was undoubtedly a great deal of agony involved, the primary motivation for hanging someone on the cross was death. The cross is a tool of demise. Jesus, therefore, declares that you must die in order to be a faithful follower of His. Death is necessary for brokenness and complete submission to His Lordship.

Brokenness addresses oneself

What precisely needs to be executed? Jesus is not referring to our physical bodies. He still demands that we carry on living for Him. Jesus is stating that each of us has to die to the self. He talks about how His genuine disciple gave up his "very self" and denied "himself."

The self: what is it? Scripture refers to it as the "flesh" at times. Not my body, but the part of me that wants to be in charge of my own life. Self-interest, or the need to be in order, is the core of sin. When he stated, "We all, like sheep, have gone astray, each of us has turned to his way; and the Lord has laid on him the iniquity of us all," the prophet Isaiah recognized this (Isaiah 53:6, italics mine). According to Roy Hession, a large "I" sits at the core of "sin."15. When God asks me to forgive, I say "no" to myself. My self is the one who attempts to hide or make excuses for my sin. It is the self that values appearances over genuine friendship and won't be honest with a brother or sister. Self opposes God and defends my behavior and mindset. Self: I think I'm better than everyone else; I believe my church, my organization, my culture, and my theology are the finest. Self belittles others and blames their sins in a self-righteous way, using their position of authority for personal gain. The one who ignores feedback and won't own up to mistakes is themselves. Self will not bow to anyone and will not concede its "rights."

"Oh, that's just the way I am" is a joint statement used by Christians. "I am unable to love that person." "I am unable to forgive that person.""I honestly can't hope to get over my anger. "I can't go and share with that brother," "I can't greet so and so," and "After all, look at what that person did to me.""That man is not my husband; you don't know who I am," I said. These words are expressions of who I am. According to Jesus, one must break oneself. One needs to die. You have to die to yourself, take up your cross, and give your life to Jesus. You have to give up and put your inner fighter to death. You jump to your defense, offering justifications for your wrong attitudes and pointing the finger or accusing others of causing them. Jesus says one must die to oneself! This self needs to be totally broken if you want Jesus to fill you fully.

Only through this death will you be able to experience the abundant Christian life. Many Christians struggle through their Christian lives needlessly, praising the Lord on the outside while letting their own will rule them on the inside.

Of course, we don't always choose to categorize self-expression as a sin. We refer to them more appropriately as "small problems," "little difficulties," or "that's just the way I am." In actuality, we struggle daily with feelings of pride, resentment, anger, rage, unforgiveness, jealousy, and more. We have to be able to identify our reflections and be prepared to label them as sin!

In Galatians, Paul talks about the manifestations of the fallen nature.

The apparent examples of wicked behavior include:

- Immorality, impurity, and debauchery in sexual matters.
- Idolatry and witchcraft.
- Hatred, strife, envy, outbursts of fury, and selfish ambition.
- Intoxication and orgies, among other things.

Before you may benefit from the remedy, you must recognize the sin in your life. Jesus offers a cure for sin, not a solution for your "little problems." If you confess your sin, Jesus' blood washes it away. I ask that there be a resurgence of people confessing their sins, that the blood of Jesus purifies and cleanses us all, that pride is crushed, that the self dies on the cross, and that Jesus' life may manifest itself in us in a fresh way.

This is the real comeback. God's power does not magically appear to bring about revival; somewhat, broken and submissive hearts and lives bear fruit. When you submit to God and receive His strength, regeneration occurs. We wonder why it takes God so long to respond to our requests. We've grown accustomed to sin. We have pardoned failed partnerships. We've argued that we're correct. However, this mindset will end our spiritual existence.

Furthermore, it will terminate the church's existence. Instead of pleading for revival, we ought to ask God to break us. We will feel resurrection then.

Paul declared, speaking from a shattered heart. I have confidence in the Son of God, who loved me and sacrificed Himself for me to sustain me in my body. (Galatians 2:20). Galatians 5:24, where he says that

Many are unwilling to incur the costs necessary for this kind of rebirth. However, you have to be prepared to bear your cross, let go of grudges, and forgive your brother or sister if you want to see the Kingdom of God come to earth. You have to approach someone and ask them to pardon you for the remarks I made about them. This is regeneration, and you will have to pay the price in full. According to John, you can only have communion with God and your brothers and sisters if you "walk in the light" (1 John 1:6-7). If

95

you are upset with a brother, you cannot have communion with God.

- Step 3: Empower others by connecting with their emotions.

It takes a connection with someone before you can affect them. You won't need to ask for aid from others or feel bad about asking for it when you have an emotional connection with them. Building relationships with others helps you understand them better, which will give you the power to influence them—especially if you're in a position of leadership. You will understand their requirements and get to know them better if you can establish an emotional connection with them. You will undoubtedly have a deeper comprehension of the people around you, which will make it easier for you to influence them. Establishing a professional rapport with others in the business world, including your staff, can facilitate the development of a flawless work environment and foster trust between you and potential clients. Given that people in this field are all unique and have various ways of thinking.

- Step 4: Honor differing viewpoints.

Above all, respect other people's opinions and consider them. Never admit you are incorrect; instead, you should always grow from your mistakes. Respecting other people's viewpoints makes them believe they are correct, which takes the focus off of you. Consider things from a different angle if someone approaches you in a professional or even personal setting and tells you that you are mistaken. Acknowledge their opinion while expressing your differing opinion. Think about asking if they'd want to hear your side of the story, but make sure you phrase it so as not to undermine their confidence. This is the most polite and effective way to persuade others if you want to share your thoughts, opinions, or perspectives.

• Step 5: Don't be a boss; instead, lead well.

Being a boss and being a leader are different things. An approachable person who makes the time to collaborate with others on ideas and projects is a leader. They even try to nudge others correctly out of respect for their dreams and ambitions. It's safe to state that a boss concentrates on self-serving interests, but a leader provides support to their subordinates and other workers. A boss needs to take the time to coordinate strategies; instead, they lead by dictating to others. These individuals typically delegate their tasks to others and only complete tasks that will help them. They frequently abuse their team members' time and don't spend any time getting to know them. You should never become a boss or behave similarly if your objective as a leader is to influence people. Regaining the respect of your business associates and coworkers is the last thing you want to happen. Communicating with and getting to know the people you work with, especially your subordinates, is the most critical aspect of being a good leader.

- Step 6: Show compassion.

React positively to people's mistakes and the idea of making mistakes itself. Never correct someone else or draw attention to their errors. Instead, you ought to instruct them on how to grow from their mistakes. It would help if you were kind and professional while offering them constructive criticism so they may grow from their mistakes and make improvements in the future. You may even issue a challenge for them to come back to you with an updated perspective on the project or whatever went wrong. They will have the chance to develop, learn, and build trust as a result. They'll ask you questions a lot more easily, and instead of giving up and admitting they failed or couldn't complete the task, they'll decide to persevere and try again until they get it right in subsequent studies. Additionally, it will instill in them the self-assurance to take pride in their work and persevere until they get it perfect. You may encourage others to develop into better versions of themselves, enhance their skills, and mature in this way.